ANIMALS AT WORK

Animals Migrating

WORLD BOOK

World Book, Inc.
180 North LaSalle Street
Suite 900
Chicago, Illinois 60601
USA

Produced for World Book, Inc. by Bailey Publishing Associates Ltd.

For information about other World Book publications, visit our website at www.worldbook.com or call 1-800-WORLDBK (967-5325).

Library of Congress Cataloging-in-Publication data has been applied for.

Title: Animals Migrating
ISBN: 978-0-7166-2735-7

Animals at Work
ISBN: 978-0-7166-2724-1 (set, hc)

Also available as:
ISBN: 978-0-7166-2748-7 (e-book)

Printed in China by Shenzhen Wing King Tong Paper Products Co, Ltd., Shenzhen, Guangdong
1st printing August 2018

0144

Staff

Writer: Alex Woolf

Executive Committee

President
Jim O'Rourke

Vice President and Editor in Chief
Paul A. Kobasa

Vice President, Finance
Donald D. Keller

Vice President, Marketing
Jean Lin

Vice President, International
Maksim Rutenberg

Vice President, Technology
Jason Dole

Director, Human Resources
Bev Ecker

Editorial

Director, Print Publishing
Tom Evans

Managing Editor
Jeff De La Rosa

Editor
William D. Adams

Manager, Contracts & Compliance
(Rights & Permissions)
Loranne K. Shields

Manager, Indexing Services
David Pofelski

Librarian
S. Thomas Richardson

Digital

Director, Digital Product Development
Erika Meller

Digital Product Manager
Jonathan Wills

Manufacturing/Production

Manufacturing Manager
Anne Fritzinger

Proofreader
Nathalie Strassheim

Graphics and Design

Senior Art Director
Tom Evans

Senior Designer
Don Di Sante

Media Editor
Rosalia Bledsoe

Special thanks to:

Roberta Bailey
Nicola Barber
Francis Paola Lea
Claire Munday
Alex Woolf

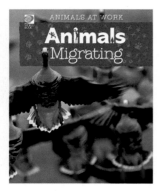

The greater white-fronted goose migrates from central and southern North America to Alaska and northern Canada to breed.

Acknowledgments

Cover photo: © Tom Reichner, Shutterstock

Alamy: Title page & 11 (WaterFrame), 6-7 (Juan-Carlos Muñoz/BIOSPHOTO), 7 (National Geographic Creative), 8 (Robert Hamilton), 9 (Steve Hamblin), 10-11 (Keith Douglas), 14-15 (Pavel Zhelev), 15 (Johnny Madsen), 20 (Thomas Groberg), 20-21 (Doug Perrine/Nature Picture Library), 23 (Murray Hayward/All Canada Photos), 25 (Norbert Wu/Minden Pictures), 28 (PureStock), 28-29 (Jelger Herder/Buiten-Beeld), 38-39 (Doug Perrine/Nature Picture Library), 39 (Shravan Sundaram), 44-45 (jspix/imageBROKER), 45 (ZUMA Press Inc). **Shutterstock**: 5 (Julian W), 6 (Andrea Izzotti), 8-9 (Delmas Lehman), 13 (Anatoliy Lukich), 16 (Melinda Fawver), 16-17 (Warren Price Photography), 17 (Joey_Danuphol), 18-19 (Protasov AN), 19 (Vladimir Wrangel), 21 (Sergey Novikov), 22-23 (Tim Robinson), 24-25 (Warren Metcalf), 27 (Rattiya Thongdumhyu), 29 (cristi180884), 30-31 (aarondfrench), 31 (Tomas Kotouc), 32-33 (JHVEPhoto), 33 (Vishnevskiy Vasily), 34-35 (FotoRequest), 35 (Neale Cousland), 37 (aaabbbccc), 41 (Oleg Znamenskiy), 42-43 (BlazingBighornStudios), 43 (iliuta goean).

Contents

4 Introduction

6 Why Animals Migrate

14 How Animals Migrate

22 Types of Migration

38 Migration Dangers

42 How People Affect Migration

46 Glossary

47 Find Out More

48 Index

Introduction

Sometimes, people move from one place to another place. They may go to a new place looking for a better life, or because they were pushed out of their old place by poverty, war, or disease. Some animals move around for many of the same reasons. They may, for example, move to get away from a natural disaster, or because their group has become too large and must spread out. These movements happen only once, for particular reasons.

Many animals also move in more regular patterns. Such a pattern of movement is called migration. Animals migrate to find food, a better climate, or a place to breed (reproduce, or make more animals like themselves). People do not usually migrate in this way today. But thousands of years ago, many groups of people migrated, following food sources and weather changes.

All types of animals migrate, including **arthropods,** birds, fish, **mammals,** and **reptiles.** Some travel thousands of miles or kilometers, while others move just a few hundred yards or meters. Some migrate every year or even every day, while others do so just once. But for all of these animals, migration is an important part of their lives. These migrating animals are also key parts of the **ecosystems** they pass through.

In this book, you will learn the reasons why animals migrate. You will read about the process of migration—how animals prepare for it and how they find their way to their destination. You will also explore the many different kinds of migration and the dangers animals face on these journeys.

How do we know about migration?

Scientists use different methods to study animal migration. One way is banding—the attaching of a small metal band to the leg of a bird. The band is engraved with a number and other information. Banding can give valuable information on the routes (paths) migrating birds take.

Radar is often used to track migrating birds and bats while they are in flight. Modern radar is powerful enough to pinpoint the animals' height, speed, and even how often they flap their wings. **Sonar** is used to track migrating fish, sea turtles, and whales.

Wildebeests migrating in the Serengeti in Africa.

Why Animals Migrate

Animals migrate because they cannot find all the resources they need in one place all year round. Warm summers may be followed by cold, harsh winters. Plants and other food sources may only be available for part of the year. The best place to breed may not necessarily be the best place to find food.

FOR FOOD

Food is a major reason for migration. As the seasons change, different areas may have more food, and animals move around to feed at the best places. An amazing example of this behavior is the annual bat migration to Kasanka National Park in the south-central African country of Zambia. From October through December, millions of straw-colored fruit bats arrive here from other parts of Africa to eat the waterberries, mango, wild loquat (*LOH kwaht),* and milkwood berries found there.

Great white sharks migrate thousands of miles or kilometers each year according to the seasonal availability of **prey.** Some spend fall off the central Californian coast, hunting the young elephant seals trying to reach the beaches at that time. The sharks then travel up to 2,500 miles (4,000 kilometers) west, to the central and eastern Pacific, where they spend the rest of the year. Researchers have found that they use fat stored in their livers as a source of energy during these long migrations.

Scientists are not sure why great white sharks make the long journey across the Pacific Ocean each year. They may do so to mate, or to find enough food.

About 10 million straw-colored fruit bats visit Kasanka every year.

Elk migration

Each spring, in Yellowstone National Park in the United States, herds of elk migrate to areas of higher altitude to eat newly sprouted grass. In the fall, when the snows arrive, the elk return to lowland **pastures,** especially wooded areas, which offer protection from cold winds. Here they eat tree bark or paw through the snow to find plants to eat. Tens of thousands of elk take part in these seasonal movements, crossing dangerous, rocky terrain and fast-moving rivers to reach their new feeding grounds.

As the winter snows melt, elk migrate to higher elevations in search of food.

FOR BETTER WEATHER

Many animals migrate to where the weather is better. But good weather is usually just an added bonus to some other reason an animal migrates. For example, birds in the Northern Hemisphere migrate south in winter partly to avoid the cold temperatures, but also because warmer places to the south give the birds a regular food supply during the winter. Some **species,** such as hummingbirds, can cope with cold temperatures as long as they have a good food supply.

The migration patterns of many shark species are partly due to changes in water temperature. The shortfin mako shark, for example, prefers to live in waters with a temperature range of 63 to 72 °F (17 to 22 °C). In early summer, when water temperatures off the northeastern coast of the United States start to rise above 63 °F (17 °C), shortfin makos will migrate there from the central North Atlantic Ocean. In November and December, when temperatures dip below 63 °F (17 °C), the sharks head back east to the open ocean.

In the Shawnee National Forest, in the central U.S. state of Illinois, snakes called water moccasins migrate each year. Along with other **reptiles** and **amphibians,** they travel east from their summer feeding grounds in the low-lying LaRue Swamp to spend the winter at the base of the Pine Hills bluffs, overlooking the Mississippi River. Wind and water have cut caves and gullies into the rock. These protect the snakes from the cold weather during their winter **hibernation.** Scientists have worked out that these migrations are mainly triggered by changes in ground temperature.

The water moccasins of Shawnee National Forest cross a road when migrating between their summer and winter habitats. The U.S. Forest Service closes the road to vehicles during the migration periods.

A flock of snow geese migrating. Each spring, they travel from as far south as Texas and Mexico to the Arctic tundra.

Hummingbird hawk moth

Butterflies and moths migrate partly to avoid bad weather, such as cold temperatures or heavy rain. They are strong flyers, battling through headwinds and flying at altitudes of several thousand feet (over a kilometer) during migration. Hummingbird hawk moths are **insects** that spend their winters in North Africa, southern Europe and southern-central Asia, and migrate to northern Europe and Russia in the summer. These patterns of migration depend on the weather. If mild weather continues past September, many moths delay their return south.

The migratory habits of the hummingbird hawk moth depend on the weather. They are more common in northern climates during hot summers.

TO REPRODUCE

Fish and other ocean animals usually migrate to eat or reproduce (to make more animals like the two that are **mating**). They do this because areas for breeding are often not ideal for feeding, and places with a lot of food may not be safe places to breed. Many fish, including striped bass, live in the sea and migrate to fresh water to **spawn.** Other **species,** such as eels, migrate from fresh water to the sea for the same reason.

Bull sharks live in **subtropical,** coastal waters all around the world. They mate and give birth in the warmest parts of their **range.** Unusually, these sharks can live in both salt water and fresh water. Females give birth in rivers, and young bull sharks grow up in coastal lagoons and river mouths where they are safer from **predators,** before migrating out to sea.

Herring are fish that migrate between their spawning, feeding, and nursery grounds in a triangular journey. For example, they might hatch off the southern coast of the northwestern European country of Norway, before migrating toward northern Norway. From there, they move on to their feeding grounds near the North Atlantic Ocean island country of Iceland, some 650 miles (1,050 kilometers) west of Norway. When they are ready to reproduce, they migrate back to their spawning grounds.

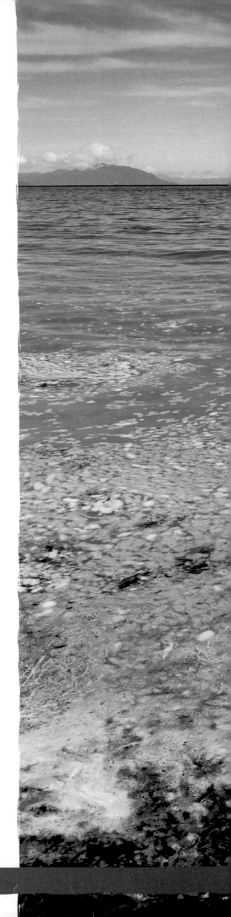

Christmas Island red crabs

A species of land crab is found almost exclusively on Christmas Island in the Indian Ocean. Once a year, the crabs leave their burrows and all migrate to the coast to breed. The migration happens in October or November, and the journey takes about a week. Males usually arrive first and dig a nest. When the females arrive, they mate with the males. The males then return inland while the females stay at the nest for another two weeks to lay their **eggs** and **incubate** them. When the eggs are ready to hatch, the female releases them into the ocean. The female then returns inland. The crab **larvae** grow in the ocean for three or four weeks before returning to shore as young crabs.

Millions of Christmas Island red crabs migrate to the coast each year to breed.

Herring spawn in Georgia Strait, near Vancouver Island in Canada.

Pacific Salmon

Pacific salmon are born and spend the early part of their lives in a freshwater lake or stream. They then migrate to the ocean where they live their adult lives, before returning to the place of their birth to **spawn.** For most Pacific salmon, this is their final journey. Those that make it usually die shortly after spawning.

The young salmon begin their journey to the ocean when they are around one or two years old. The current carries them downstream, as their bodies go through changes to allow them to survive in saltwater. The journey can be hundreds or even thousands of miles or kilometers in length. Many are eaten by fish and birds or killed by polluted water before they reach the ocean.

Adult salmon live in the ocean from six months to seven years, mostly eating shrimp, squid, and smaller fish. Their bodies again change in preparation for their journey upriver, for example by adding muscle that can be used for quick bursts of speed. In their migration, which can take several months, the fish must battle strong currents, swim through rapids, and even leap up waterfalls. Many scientists think salmon use their strong sense of smell to guide them back to their birthplace.

Many salmon die during the journey. Fishing crews catch some and others are killed by pollution. They are also vulnerable to **predators,** such as bears, bald eagles, otters, and sea lions. Sometimes, their progress is halted by dams. Cement staircases called fish ladders have been built next to some dams to help salmon get over them, but many are so weakened by the process that they die from exhaustion.

The salmon that manage to survive the journey look different from when they started out. The males have humped backs and hooked jaws. The females are swollen with **eggs.** Both sexes have white bruises on their skin and tears in their fins from their difficult journey. The females build a nest and lay their eggs, and males **fertilize** them. Their journey complete, most of the parents die, exhausted. The eggs hatch after two to four months, and the cycle begins again.

SALMON
swimming
upriver

How Animals Migrate

Migration is a physically challenging activity in the lives of many **species.** They have to prepare themselves before making these journeys and find food along the way. They must find their way to distant destinations, sometimes in large groups, sometimes alone. Animals have come up with many different ways of surviving the challenges of migration.

TRIGGERS

How do animals know when to migrate? Seasonal changes, such as shorter days, cooling temperatures, and shrinking food supplies, can trigger migrations. Monarch butterflies, for example, begin to migrate in the fall when they sense that the days are getting shorter. These environmental changes cause the bodies of migratory birds, fish, **amphibians,** and **insects** to make special **hormones.** The hormones trigger changes in their bodies to help them prepare for the journey ahead

PREPARATION

Many migrant animals eat a lot before departing, building up fat to give them a source of energy during their journey. Animals that do this include birds, dragonflies, caribou (*KAR uh boo),* and whales. Birds that migrate long distances often double their body weight before setting off. Birds go through other physical changes, too. They strengthen their muscles and shed old feathers so new ones can grow. In some species, such as sparrows, vireos, warblers, and godwits, the sizes of their **organs** change: their heart and flight muscles get bigger and their digestive organs shrink.

Bar-tailed godwit

The bar-tailed godwit is a large wading bird. Its migration route includes a flight of 7,100 miles (11,500 kilometers) from the far northwest U.S. state of Alaska to the Pacific Ocean island country of New Zealand. The bird makes this flight without stopping for food, water, or rest, making it the longest nonstop flight of any known bird. The godwit uses its long beak to pull **invertebrates,** such as crabs and worms, from the mud of sea shores. It eats constantly to prepare for the flight, doubling its weight from around 10 ½ to 21 ounces (300 to 600 grams). Its stomach, liver, kidneys, and intestines shrink to make room for the extra fat. Godwits also replace their flight feathers with new ones strong enough to withstand the long flight.

A bar-tailed godwit in flight. Each year, thousands of these birds make an epic, nonstop journey across the Pacific Ocean.

A monarch butterfly feeds in Canada before migrating south for the winter.

MIGRATION ROUTES

Most bird migration happens in the Northern Hemisphere because it has more land than the Southern Hemisphere. Birds generally fly south to warmer places in winter and north to cooler climates in spring. Many **species** of bird migrate along regular routes called flyways. These routes are not usually direct, but usually follow coastlines and rivers, and pass over good places to rest and eat. Flyways also avoid geographical barriers, such as mountains. Most land birds avoid seas and large lakes because there is not enough food for them over these huge bodies of water. Water birds avoid large stretches of land without water for the same reason.

Scientists have learned much about the flyways of water birds. Less is known about the routes of land birds, which usually fly at night and **roost** and eat during the day. What scientists do know is that land birds generally take different routes in spring and fall to make use of seasonal patterns in weather, wind direction, and food. For example, rufous hummingbirds follow the coast in spring, from Mexico to Alaska, but take an inland route when flying south in fall, to drink the sugary liquid called nectar made by mountain wildflowers. In North America, there are four major flyways for migrating birds—the Pacific, Central, Mississippi, and Atlantic.

Scientists think that up to 50 out of some 5,200 known dragonfly species migrate. In some ways, their migratory behavior is like that of birds. For example, dragonflies build up fat reserves before they migrate (see pages 14-15) and can get back on course if blown off track (see pages 18-19). They also follow the same flyways as birds. Also like birds, dragonflies stop about once every three days to rest and eat. Unlike birds, no single dragonfly survives to complete a round trip. It is their offspring that make the return journey.

The green darner dragonfly follows the same flyway as the bird called the American kestrel, migrating south along Lake Superior during September. Kestrels eat these dragonflies to get some nourishment while migrating.

A flock of Canada geese migrating along the Mississippi flyway.

Emperor penguins on the march. Even though emperor penguins live in different parts of Antarctica, they all migrate at the same time.

Emperor penguin

Every March, emperor penguins of Antarctica make the difficult journey from their feeding grounds at the coast to their breeding grounds inland. They cross 60 to 100 miles (100 to 160 kilometers) of ice by walking and sliding along on their bellies. The route changes each year because the shifting ice puts new obstacles in the way, such as walls of ice and deep chasms called crevasses (*kruh VA sehz).*

FINDING THEIR WAY

Migrating animals use different methods to find their way. They may be guided by landforms, such as coasts, rivers, and hills. Or they may work out their route from the position of the sun, moon, and stars. This takes an internal clock, since such objects move over the course of the day. When clouds hide the sun, many animals can still find their way by seeing polarized light coming through the clouds. Polarized light waves vibrate in simple, regular patterns. By sensing how this light is polarized, these animals can work out where the sun is behind the clouds.

Fish find their way with the help of ocean currents and changes in water temperature and salt levels. Some scientists think that salmon, trout, and eels use Earth's **magnetic field** to guide them across the ocean. When water crosses the magnetic field, it creates a weak electric current that fishes may sense. Salmon may use their sense of smell to help them find their way back to the stream where they were born. Sea lampreys are drawn to suitable streams for **spawning** by a **pheromone** given off by previous generations of baby lampreys.

Scientists do not know exactly how migrating birds fly the same routes year after year, but they manage to do so with amazing accuracy. Researchers studying a **colony** of common terns found that more than 80 percent of them returned to nest less than 26 feet (8 meters) from their nest from the year before.

Young birds may learn the route from their parents, and they may remember landmarks. They may also be helped by an internal compass: a bird's eyes work with its brain to figure out which way is north. A nerve connecting the bird's beak to its brain can sense the strength of Earth's magnetic field. The magnetic field gets weaker closer to the equator, so a bird might be able to combine this information with other clues to work out where it is. Some experts think birds' sense of smell can help them find their way.

Loggerhead sea turtles

Loggerhead sea turtles migrate some 1,400 miles (2,300 kilometers) between their feeding and nesting grounds, but can find their way even as hatchlings making their first journey. They can do this because they are born with an internal magnetic map. Earth's magnetic field varies in different parts of the globe. These differences act like road signs in the sea. As the turtle reaches them, it changes direction so that it stays on course.

The remarkable skills of the loggerhead sea turtle help it avoid waters that are too cold. It also knows how to find currents to carry it in the direction it wants to go to save energy.

Migrating birds will often use landmarks, such as river valleys, to figure out where they are.

TRAVELING ALONE OR IN GROUPS

Animals migrate in different ways. Most migrate together for protection or to save energy. With more traveling partners, the group is more likely to quickly spot a potential **predator** and react. But some animals, such as sea turtles and the solitary sandpiper (a shorebird), migrate alone.

NIGHT AND DAY

Some birds migrate during the day. They include large birds, like vultures, buzzards, eagles, and storks, which can soar on columns of rising warm air called thermals. Such thermals only form during daylight hours. Swifts and swallows also migrate by day and eat flying **insects** as they go. But many songbirds, including warblers, thrushes, and starlings, migrate mostly at night. The air usually is calmer and cooler, so they can save energy by flapping less. There are also fewer predators around.

FORMATION

Spiny lobsters sometimes migrate in long, straight lines across the ocean floor, using their **antennae** to keep in touch with the lobster in front. These migrations can last several days and nights without stopping. The lobsters will usually continue in a straight line even when facing currents or obstacles on the sea floor. Scientists think these groupings help reduce **drag** and enable the lobsters to protect each other from predators.

Many migrating birds fly in a V-shaped group to save energy. Experiments with pelicans have shown that their heart rate is lower when they fly in this formation than when flying alone. Each bird flies slightly above the one in front, to make use of the upward-moving air—called upwash—created by the other bird's wingtips. The birds time their wingbeats to the coming of the upwash, giving them extra lift.

A flock of swans flying in V formation. Birds take it in turns to be at the front, falling back when they get tired.

Elephant migration

African elephants migrate seasonally in search of food and water. The size of migrant groups varies. Sometimes individual family groups migrate alone, usually when there is not enough food to support a larger herd. At other times, several family groups join to form a "bond group" and migrate together. Traveling in a bond group is safer, but takes more food. Once in a while, elephant groups combine to form large migratory herds. This gives the most security against predators, but can only work if much food is available along the migration route.

A family of migrating African elephants. Adults travel in the front and rear to protect the young from predators.

A line of spiny lobsters migrating from their nursery to their feeding grounds.

Types of Migration

Migrations take many forms. They can involve very long or very short trips and be in different directions. Most birds, for example, migrate from north to south and back, but some move between eastern and western **ranges.** Other animals migrate up and down hillsides, or between waters near coasts and the deeper ocean.

SEASONAL MIGRATION

Many animals migrate back and forth every year between their summer and winter ranges. For example, the southern right whale travels to the waters of Antarctica for feeding during the summer. The whales spend their winters in warmer waters along the coasts of South America, southern Africa, and Australia, where they **mate** and the mothers give birth.

Hoofed **mammals** called pronghorns take part in the longest land mammal migration in North America. A group of pronghorns spend winters in the Upper Green River Valley, in the western U.S. state of Wyoming. With the coming of spring, the group travels north to its summer range in Grand Teton National Park. The group makes the return trip south in the fall before the snow blocks its path through the Gros Ventre Mountains.

DIFFERENT DIRECTIONS

Most kinds of animal migrate from north to south and back again. This is called **latitudinal** (*lat uh TOO duh nuhl*) **migration.** They move to warmer areas (southward in the Northern Hemisphere, northward in the Southern Hemisphere) during the winter, and cooler places in the summer. But some birds migrate from east to west and back again. This is called **longitudinal** (*lon juh TOO duh nuhl*) **migration.** For example, many common starlings migrate toward the Atlantic coast from Eastern Europe and western Asia to avoid the harsh winter there.

Molt migrations

Many **species** of waterfowl migrate every year before their molting periods. This is a time when birds shed their old, worn feathers to replace them with new ones. Unlike most birds, waterfowl replace their wing, tail, and body feathers all at once. They cannot fly during these periods, making them easy **prey** to **predators.** They must also eat lots of protein-rich food so their new feathers are not thin or poorly formed. For these reasons, many ducks, geese, and swans make a molt migration. This takes place before they molt, in the summer, and they migrate to wetlands further north. Here they face fewer predators, and the long daylight hours allow lots of time for searching for food.

This male Wilson's phalarope (FAL uh rohp) has molted and is now showing its winter coloring. It will soon fly south from Alberta, Canada, to spend the winter in South America.

ALTITUDINAL MIGRATION

Some animals migrate up and down hillsides each year. They do this because of seasonal changes in the weather and the availability of food at different elevations. This is called **altitudinal** (*al tuh TOO duh nuhl*) **migration.** Sometimes, they may move for safety. For example, bighorn sheep of North America spend their summers high up in the mountains where they are safer from **predators,** such as bears, wolves, and cougars. In winter, they move down to lower elevations where there is more food.

The white-ruffed manakin is a fruit-eating bird of Central America. Manakins in Costa Rica spend their breeding season in forests at heights of around 1,800 feet (550 meters). From August to October, many of them migrate to lower-elevation forests as fruit gets harder to find

BETWEEN THE COAST AND THE OCEAN

Many **species** of **arthropods,** such as crab, lobster, and shrimp, migrate between waters at the coasts and the deeper ocean each year. Lobsters may move up to 6 miles (10 kilometers) per year. They stay close to shore in the spring and summer, and move to deeper waters in late fall. Tagging and tracking studies have shown large lobsters living in deep canyons off the New England coast. Why they go there is not known, but some lobster fishers claim it is a lobster breeding ground.

Brown shrimp are found in the western Atlantic and Gulf of Mexico. In the autumn and winter, the shrimp move their **larvae** to shallow, coastal waters and estuaries. In late spring and early summer, the adult brown shrimp return to deeper, saltier water. The young shrimp make this journey when they are grown. (An estuary [*EHS chu EHR ee*] is a river opening at the sea coast where salt and fresh waters mix.)

Swarming crabs

The pelagic red crab lives in the eastern Pacific Ocean. It mostly lives in the waters near to shore, but sometimes migrates to deeper waters, possibly to avoid predators. (*Pelagic [puh LAJ ihk]* means *of the ocean*.) In warmer weather, the population can suddenly swell, and huge **swarms** of them have migrated across the sea floor.

Huge numbers of migrating pelagic red crabs have been washed up on this beach in Baja California, Mexico.

Bighorn sheep migrate each year between higher and lower altitudes.

Daily Movement

The biggest migration on the planet, in terms of the number of living things involved, happens every single day. This is the vertical (up-and-down) movement of tiny animals called **zooplankton** (*ZOH uh plangk tuhn*) between the lower and upper levels of lakes, seas, and oceans. The zooplankton move toward the surface at dusk, and return to deeper waters before dawn. This is called diel vertical migration. *Diel* comes from the Latin word for *day* and means "a 24-hour period."

Diel vertical migration costs these tiny animals a great deal of energy, so why do they do it? Zooplankton come to the surface to eat tiny plants living in the upper waters. They come at night because they are less likely to be eaten by **predators.** Most of their predators are fish that hunt near the surface using sight, so the zooplankton return to deeper, darker water during the day. They are safer here, though deep-water predators such as jellyfish, that do not hunt by sight still can catch them.

Zooplankton might also make the daily migration to avoid the harmful effects of **ultraviolet** rays from the sun. Zooplankton are harmed by ultraviolet rays, so they avoid being too close to the surface during daylight hours.

ZOOPLANKTON seen under a microscope.

What triggers diel vertical migration? It may be changes in the strength of daylight. When the zooplankton sense light dimming, they start to rise, and when they sense it brightening, they start to descend. But this does not explain how the migration is triggered among deep-sea zooplankton that live at depths beyond which sunlight can penetrate. One possibility is that zooplankton, like migrating birds, have an internal clock that tells them when to rise and when to fall. The clock would have to change with the seasons to match the changing times of sunrise and sunset.

SHORT-DISTANCE MIGRATION

Amphibians, including salamanders and frogs, migrate short distances of between a few yards or meters and a few miles or kilometers. They move between ponds, streams, and swamps for breeding and **spawning,** and special places where they **hibernate.** These seasonal movements may also include periods spent at special feeding areas. Amphibians have thin skin that quickly loses moisture in hot, dry conditions. For this reason, migrations usually are short. Amphibians also often migrate at night or when it is raining to prevent their skin from drying out.

Their migration routes often lead them across rough terrain, including dense (thick) brush and long grass. But their strong directional sense allows them to find their way back to their breeding ponds. Their routes sometimes lead them across busy roads, causing many deaths. Local authorities may build special tunnels so the amphibians can cross safely beneath the roads.

Not many bats migrate—only about 30 of the more than 1,000 **species.** Unlike birds, which migrate to make use of seasonal changes in food supply, bats usually migrate to find better conditions for hibernation. As a result, many bats only migrate short distances. A group of Virginia big-eared bats in the southeastern U.S. state of North Carolina migrates just 8 miles (13 kilometers) between its summer and winter **roosts.**

The big brown bat, which lives in North and Central America, spends its summers roosting in hollow trees, cracks in rocks, or the eaves of attics and barns. In the winter, it roosts in caves and underground mines, where temperatures are constant. It usually migrates less than 25 miles (40 kilometers), although distances of 143 miles (230 kilometers) have been recorded.

A group of hibernating Virginia big-eared bats.

Salamanders

Each spring, salamanders in the northeastern U.S. state of Massachusetts leave their winter hibernation zones in wooded upland areas. They migrate to vernal pools to breed. Vernal pools are small ponds that form each spring from melting snow and spring rains. The pools are temporary—by mid-summer they have dried up—so they are free of **predators.** The salamanders go to the pools early in spring, usually in March, to give their young time to grow before the pool dries up.

Spotted salamanders are among the most common salamander species at vernal pools in Massachusetts.

A European common frog on the lookout during migration.

LONG-DISTANCE MIGRATION

Some animals migrate huge distances, sometimes thousands of miles or kilometers every year. Such animals have a strong directional sense and a lot of energy. They can survive and repair the harm done to their bodies by traveling such long distances.

The Arctic tern, a type of seabird, covers a greater distance than any other known animal in its annual migration, with journeys of up to 56,000 miles (90,000 kilometers). Its breeding grounds are in the Arctic and northern temperate (not very hot or cold) areas of North America, Europe, and Asia. It spends the summer there, then flies in a winding path to the south, reaching the Antarctic coast in time for the southern summer. Because of this migration pattern, this bird experiences two summers each year and more daylight than any other creature on the planet.

Sea turtles make long-distance migrations of sometimes thousands of miles or kilometers between nesting beaches and feeding grounds. The leatherback sea turtle is the largest of all sea turtle **species** and travels the farthest in its migrations. One group of female leatherbacks lays its **eggs** on tropical beaches in Indonesia and other parts of the western Pacific. The turtles then migrate across the ocean basin to their feeding grounds, including places off the coasts of California or southeastern Australia, where they hunt for jellyfish. Scientists attached a radio device to one female leatherback on its journey across the Pacific and part of the way back again. It covered at least 12,744 miles (20,509 kilometers) before the signal was lost.

Humpback whales

Among the longest known **mammal** migrations is that of the humpback whale. Humpbacks feed in polar waters and migrate to tropical or **subtropical** zones to breed. Populations of humpbacks in the North Pacific leave their summer waters around Alaska in the fall, arriving six to eight weeks later around Hawaii where they spend the winter. Here they **mate,** and the mothers give birth and raise their calves before returning north in the spring, a round trip of about 6,000 miles (9,500 kilometers).

A humpback whale calf. The longest recorded journey by a humpback whale was 11,706 miles (18,839 kilometers), from the island of American Samoa to the Antarctic Peninsula.

GENERATIONAL MIGRATION

Many kinds of **insects,** especially dragonflies, butterflies, moths, and beetles, make mass migrations. Often, the ones that set out on the migration do not live to reach the destination, let alone make the return journey. Sometimes, it takes several generations of insects to complete the round trip. Migrating insects behave differently than insects that are not migrating: they fly straighter and with more purpose and ignore things along the way that nonmigrating insects would react to, such as **predators,** rivals, or **mates.**

Among the most amazing of all insect migrations is the epic yearly journey of the monarch butterfly across North America. Each fall, millions of these butterflies travel up to 2,970 miles (4,750 kilometers) from southern Canada and the northern United States to Mexico and the southern part of the western U.S. state of California.

Monarch butterflies migrate south because they cannot survive the cold winters in the north. They make the return journey because the plants their **larvae** need to eat do not grow where they spend their winters. They must fly back north to where the plants can be found. No single individual lives to complete the round trip. Instead, the females lay **eggs** during the northward migration, from which hatches the next generation of migrants.

The butterflies find their way using the sun. Their eyes track the position of the sun in the sky, while special structures in their **antennae** keep track of the time of day. By comparing these two signals, they can work out their position and direction and stay on course.

Globe skimmer

The globe skimmer dragonfly makes the longest migration of any insect. It makes a round trip of between 8,700 and 11,200 miles (14,000 and 18,000 kilometers) from the southern part of the south Asian country of India to the Maldives, a chain of islands in the western Indian Ocean, and then on to eastern and southern Africa. It takes four generations to complete the migration. Researchers think the dragonflies make use of high-altitude winds to go on these epic journeys. Dragonflies breed in temporary rainwater pools, so they may be making use of weather systems that bring rains to India and, later in the year, to eastern and southern Africa.

A globe skimmer dragonfly.

Monarch butterflies roost on a tree in Mexico. They spend the winter hibernating in trees. Remarkably, monarchs return to the same trees each year, even though they are different individuals than were there the previous year.

IRREGULAR MOVEMENTS

Once in a while, large groups of animals move in ways that are not guided by seasonal or daily cycles. Instead, they move in respose to unusual conditions, such as strange weather or a sudden growth of the food supply. These movements care called irruptions. Many kinds of animals irrupt, but irruptions are seen most often among birds.

The red-breasted nuthatch is a songbird that eats seeds and **insects.** It normally spends its winters near the Canadian-U.S. border, but in the winter of 2016–17 it turned up much farther south, from Los Angeles, California, to Tampa, Florida. The nuthatches likely irrupted because the pine trees in the forests of Canada and the northern United States produced many more seeds than usual in 2016. With all this extra food, the birds bred earlier and had more offspring. Because there were so many young nuthatches, many had to fly south in search of food during the winter.

There can be big changes in the numbers of painted lady butterflies. A rainy spring can cause many plants that their caterpillars eat to grow. Unlike monarch caterpillars, painted lady caterpillars can eat many kinds of plants, so they can spread widely during these irruptions.

NOMADIC MOVEMENTS

Scientists call some bird **species** nomadic rather than migratory, because their movements are unpredictable and depend on the availability of food and water sources. Nomadic birds usually stay in the same geographic **range,** but the areas where they breed and spend the winter may change from year to year, depending on food supplies. Nomadic birds include the Bohemian waxwing, which continually moves around during winter in search of fruit and berries. Phainopeplas *(fay Y noh PEHP luhz),* desert birds of southwestern North America, are also nomads, moving in flocks to find suitable nesting or fruiting trees.

Emus

The emu is a large, flightless bird that lives on the continent of Australia. It is a nomadic bird, moving throughout its **range** in search of plants and insects to eat. Emus are well-suited to this lifestyle. They can move for long periods at a fast trot, need little water, and can go for weeks without eating. This allows them to travel great distances to find food.

Emus can tolerate a wide range of temperatures, which helps them in their nomadic lifestyle.

In 2013-14, there was an irruption of snowy owls. Due to a boom in the population of lemmings, their favorite prey, many of them showed up a long way south of their usual range.

Locusts

Locusts are a name given to about a dozen **species** of grasshopper that sometimes gather into **swarms.** These swarms can be huge, made up of billions of individuals spread over an area of thousands of square miles or kilometers. They are also dense, with up to 200 million locusts packed into a square mile (80 million per square kilometer). Each locust can eat its own weight in plants per day, so swarms can devastate crops and destroy the livelihoods of farmers. Locust swarms, called plagues, can happen in many parts of the world, especially North Africa, the Middle East, India, and Australia.

Locusts usually live alone, but under special conditions their behavior changes. Where locusts live, heavy rainfall can cause many green plants to grow for a short time. Locust populations may explode because of the large amount of available food. During the dry weather that follows, the normally timid **insects** are forced closer together on ever-smaller patches of plants. As they touch each other's rear legs, their bodies give off a **hormone** that triggers changes in how they look and behave. Such locusts eat much more and breed more often. They also grow bigger and change color. For example, one species, the desert locust, becomes darker with contrasting yellow and black markings.

These swarming locusts form into small bands. Such an event is called an outbreak. If conditions cause bands to join together in larger groups, the event is called an upsurge. When upsurges from different breeding areas come together, it is called a plague. As the locusts move across the landscape, they stop to eat. After the leading locusts settle on an area of plants, the ones behind them fly over and settle farther on. In this way, the swarm moves in a rolling motion with changing leaders. Swarms can cover huge distances. In 1954, a swarm flew from northwest Africa to the United Kingdom.

A swarm of LOCUSTS in Madagascar.

Migration Dangers

Migrating animals face many dangers on their journeys, such as hunger, exhaustion, bad weather, and **predators.** There is also the risk of disease when large groups of animals come together. Such diseases can devastate bird populations when migrating flocks carry an illness to a larger **colony. Amphibian** migrants can become dehydrated—have too little moisture—if they spend too long in hot, dry weather. Droughts, storms, and wildfires can destroy food sources for migrating animals.

PREDATORS

From May to July, billions of small fish called sardines migrate northward along the eastern coast of southern Africa. Their large numbers attract predators. Dolphins are often first on the scene, herding the sardines toward the surface. The frightened sardines form into dense, swirling masses called bait balls, with each fish trying to reach the center of the ball. Bait balls are soon spotted by other predators, such as sharks, Cape gannets (a type of seabird), and whales. This usually triggers a feeding frenzy as the ball is attacked from all sides.

Eleonora's falcon, which breeds on islands in the Mediterranean Sea, hunts migrating birds. Small birds reach the islands in late summer and early fall on their way south. Eleonora's falcon delays breeding until late summer so it can use the migrating birds as a food source for its hatchlings. The falcon patrols the coastal cliffs, using its speed and agility to catch the tired migrants in mid-flight. It removes its **prey's** wing and tail feathers so it cannot fly away and imprisons it in a hole or jams it into a tight space between rocks. The falcon may leave a prey animal imprisoned this way for up to a few days before returning to kill it and feed it to the falcon's young.

Bad weather

Bad weather can affect migrating birds. Storms at sea can throw birds into the waves where they drown. Sandstorms and fog can confuse birds, causing them to drift off course. Birds that lose their way are called vagrants. In 1967, a black-browed albatross from the South Atlantic wound up in Scotland, in the northern part of Great Britain, some 8,000 miles (12,800 kilometers) from its normal breeding grounds, where it made its home in a colony of gannets.

This red-necked stint, from the western Pacific, got blown off course during migration and ended up in the San Francisco Bay area of California.

Dolphins attacking a sardine bait ball off the coast of South Africa.

The Great Wildebeest Migration

One of the world's most amazing migrations is the movement of wildebeests and other grazing **mammals** through Africa's Serengeti plain. More than two million animals, including over a million wildebeests and hundreds of thousands of antelopes and zebras, take part in a journey that loops between the Serengeti National Park in the eastern African country of Tanzania and the Maasai Mara National Reserve in the east-central country of Kenya. There is no start or end point of this migration—the animals move as the seasons change in their constant search for fresh grazing land and water. The journey is dangerous. **Predators,** such as cheetahs, crocodiles, hyenas, and lions, hunt the migrants, and many drown while trying to cross lakes and rivers.

In January and February, the wildebeest females give birth on the **savannas** of the southern Serengeti. Some 300,000 to 400,000 calves are born over the course of two to three weeks. The young are up on their feet and running with the herd minutes after their birth. Even so, many die in their first year, killed by predators, starvation, exhaustion, or disease. Many get separated from their mothers during chaotic lake and river crossings. Lost calves are easy **prey** for any watching predators.

In March, toward the end of the short dry season, the grass begins to dry out and the wildebeests head west across the plains, following the rains and the growth of new grass. In April, the herds start migrating north. The **mating** season happens in May and June, during the journey north, as males compete to mate with the females. The herd continues north during July and August, following the rains into the greener **pastures** of the Maasai Mara. In September, they face their toughest challenge: crossing the mighty Mara River.

The herds start heading south again in late October, reaching the southern Serengeti in late November and December. Then the great cycle begins again.

WILDEBEEST grazing in the Maasai Mara

How People Affect Migration

Human activity has had a huge impact on all animal **species,** whether they migrate or not. But the impact on migratory species is often greater, because they have more than one **habitat.** For example, if the habitat in which a species spends the winter is destroyed, the population may decline, even if its breeding grounds and stopover areas are unharmed. Major human threats to migratory animals include habitat destruction and **global warming.**

HABITAT DESTRUCTION

Agriculture, deforestation, mining, and overfishing are all examples of human activities that can harm the habitats of migrating animals. For example, European songbirds have lost much of their winter habitat in North Africa due to overgrazing and growing deserts. In East Africa, farmland is spreading into the migratory routes of wildebeests, zebras, and elephants. Illegal logging in Michoacán (*mee choh ah CAHN),* a state on the Pacific coast of Mexico, is destroying the forests where the monarch butterflies of eastern North America spend the winter.

The cerulean (*suh ROO lee uhn)* warbler has suffered at both ends of its migratory route. Mountaintop-removal mining has destroyed large areas of its breeding habitat in the forests of eastern North America. And the forests on the slopes of the South American Andes, where it winters, are being cleared for agriculture.

Before Europeans came to the Pacific coast of North America, some 67 to 95 million salmon migrated each year up the rivers of what are now the western U.S. states of Washington, Oregon, Idaho, and California. Today, because of dam construction, overfishing, logging, and water pollution, the salmon populations there have declined to just 5 to 6 million.

Curlew sandpiper

Curlew sandpipers, migratory shorebirds of East Asia and Australasia, are suffering from habitat destruction at their stopover areas. The birds used to rest and feed at the tidal flats of the Yellow Sea near China and the Korean Peninsula. But due to growth of industry on the flats, pollution, and the invasion of non-native grasses, they are no longer a suitable habitat for the birds. They are forced to fly on, exhausted, and many die during their migration.

Due to habitat destruction and hunting, curlew sandpiper numbers are dropping by around 10 percent each year, and the species is threatened with extinction.

In Montana, bison migrate along river valleys in winter in search of food. They are sometimes killed by ranchers due to fears they might spread disease to their cattle.

GLOBAL WARMING

Global warming is the rise in Earth's average surface temperature since the mid-1800's. There is strong evidence that humans have caused most of this warming since the mid-1900's, due to such activities as the burning of coal in power plants and gasoline in automobiles.

Global warming is the biggest cause of **climate change.** Climate change is a difference in the usual weather of a particular place. Climate change has already upset the migratory behavior of many different animals. For example, many songbirds in Europe and North America time their breeding season to the coming out of caterpillars and other **insects,** which the birds then feed to their young. Warming temperatures have led to caterpillars hatching earlier in the season, before the birds have returned from their winter homes to the south, leaving their chicks without enough to eat.

Scientists also blame climate change for a decline in the numbers of migrating wildebeests and other grazers on the Serengeti. As the Indian Ocean warms, it changes weather patterns over East Africa. These changing patterns result in both more rain and drought, upsetting the timings of the migration.

WHAT IF MIGRATION STOPPED?

The sight of huge flocks, **schools, swarms,** or herds of migrating animals can be beautiful, but migration is far more than an impressive sight. Migrating animals also play valuable parts in the **ecosystems** they pass through. Migrating songbirds eat caterpillars that would otherwise eat the leaves of trees and shrubs. Migrating butterflies also perform a valuable service at their stopover areas by **pollinating** flowers as they gather nectar. Pacific salmon move **nutrients** from the ocean onto land through their migration. As adult salmon travel upstream, such **predators** as eagles and bears catch them. If the salmon disappeared or stopped migrating, the link from the sea to the coast would be broken, and predator numbers would decline because there would not be enough food.

All these animals make important contributions to the environment as they move from place to place. The challenge is to allow them to keep doing so in a world with more and more people taking up more and more space.

Sea turtles

The migratory instincts (something an animal was born knowing how to do) of sea turtles take them back to the same beaches year after year to lay their **eggs.** But due to rising sea levels, another impact of global warming, many of these beaches are disappearing. Global warming is also probably causing a greater number of strong storms, which have washed away more nesting beaches and flooded more sea turtle nests.

Erosion on this Florida beach has exposed the eggs of a loggerhead sea turtle.

The Cape gannet is a migratory waterbird theatened by climate change, as its fish prey may not be able to survive warming seas.

Glossary

agriculture the raising of plants and animals for human benefit.

altitudinal migration migration between higher and lower altitudes, such as up and down a mountain.

amphibian a vertebrate with scaleless skin that usually lives part of its life in water and part on land. Vertebrate animals have a backbone.

antenna (plural antennae) a long, delicate sense organ, or feeler, found on the heads of various invertebrates, including insects.

arthropod a very large group of invertebrates that includes insects, arachnids, and crustaceans.

climate change a change in the usual weather of a particular place, often associated with global warming.

colony a group of living things of one species that live together or grow in the same place.

drag the force that pushes against an object when it moves through air or water, slowing it down.

ecosystem a system made up of a group of living things and its physical environment, and the relationship between them.

egg a female sex cell, or the structure in which the embryo develops, usually outside the mother's body.

fertilize to join sperm from a male with egg from a female so that a young animal develops.

global warming a worldwide rise in temper-atures, caused by air pollution.

habitat the place where a living thing usually makes its home.

hibernate, hibernation to spend the winter in a state like deep sleep. Breathing, heart rate, and other body processes slow down.

hormone a chemical produced in a living thing to bring about changes in its cells and body parts.

incubate to keep fertilized eggs warm so that the embryos develop properly and hatch.

insect one of the major invertebrate groups. Insects have six legs and a three-part body.

invertebrate an animal without a backbone.

larva (plural larvae) the active, immature stage of some animals, such as many insects, that is different from its adult form.

latitudinal migration migration between latitudes—regions north or south of, and parallel to, the equator.

longitudinal migration migration between longitudes—imaginary lines that run north and south along the Earth's surface. Such migrations move between east and west.

magnetic field a region around a magnetic material or a moving electric charge within which the force of magnetism acts.

mammal one of the major vertebrate animal groups. Vertebrate animals have a backbone. Mammals feed their offspring on milk produced by the mother, and most have hair or fur.

mate the animal with which another animal partners to reproduce (to make more animals like the two that are mating); the act of mating, when two animals come together to reproduce.

nutrient a substance that is needed to keep a living thing alive and help it grow.

organ a part of the body, made of similar cells and cell tissue, that performs a particular function.

pasture land covered with grass that is suitable for feeding animals.

pheromone a chemical substance linked to the sense of smell given out by an animal as a signal to others in its species.

pollinate to put pollen into a flower or plant so that it produces seeds.

predator an animal that hunts, kills, and eats other animals.

prey an animal that is hunted, killed, and eaten by another.

Find Out More

radar a system for detecting the presence, direction, distance, and speed of objects. It works by sending out pulses of radio waves, which are reflected off the object back to the source.

range the area in which a species can be found.

reptile one of the major vertebrate animal groups. Vertebrate animals have a backbone. A reptile has dry, scaly skin and breathes air. Snakes, crocodiles, and lizards are all reptiles.

roost a place where a group of animals, particularly birds, regularly sleeps; the act of roosting.

savanna grasslands with widely scattered bushes and trees.

school in fish, to move together in a large group through the water; a group of fish moving together through the water.

sonar a system for detecting objects underwater by giving off sound pulses, which are reflected off the object back to the source.

spawn to lay and fertilize eggs in water.

species a group of living things that have certain permanent traits in common and are able to reproduce with each other.

subtropical describing the areas bordering the tropics.

swarm a large group of arthropods moving together either in search of food or a new home.

ultraviolet rays a form of light not visible to humans. Ultraviolet rays lie just beyond the violet end of the visible spectrum. The sun is a major source of ultraviolet rays.

zooplankton tiny animals that drift at or near the surface of oceans, lakes, and other water bodies.

BOOKS

Animal Migration (Spotlight on Ecology and Life Science) by Holden Straus (PowerKids Press, 2017)

The Incredible Migration of Monarch Butterflies (Stories from the Wild Animal Kingdom) by Nancy Furstinger (Momentum, 2018)

Thousand-Mile Fliers and Other Amazing Migrators (Searchlight Books Animal Superpowers) by Rebecca E. Hirsch (Lerner, 2017)

WEBSITES

BBC Nature Wildlife – Migration
http://www.bbc.co.uk/nature/adaptations/Animal_migration
Learn about and watch videos of some of the world's most amazing animal migrations.

National Geographic – Epic Animal Migrations in Yellowstone
http://video.nationalgeographic.com/video/magazine/160401-ngm-yellowstone-national-park-migrations
Watch a video of some of the awesome migrations that take place each year in the Greater Yellowstone Ecosystem.

The Nature Education Knowledge Project – Animal Migration
https://www.nature.com/scitable/knowledge/library/animal-migration-13259533
Find out all about animal migration—what it is, why and how it happens, and how we know about it.

PBS Nova – Magnetic Attraction
http://www.pbs.org/wgbh/nova/nature/magnetic-impact-on-animals.html
Discover out how animals use Earth's magnetic field to find their way during migration.

Index

altitudinal migration 7, 24–25
amphibians 8, 14, 28–29, 38
Arctic terns 30–31

bar-tailed godwit 15
bats 4, 6–7, 28
    big brown bat 28
bighorn sheep 24–25
birds 4, 8–9, 12–13, 14, 15,
    16–17, 18–19, 20, 22, 23, 24,
    27, 30–31, 34–35, 38, 39. 42,
    43, 44
bison 43
breeding, migration for 4, 6, 10–13,
    17, 22, 24, 28, 29, 30, 31
brown shrimp 24
butterflies 9, 14–15, 32–33, 34, 44
    monarch butterfly 14–15,
        32–33
    painted lady butterflies 34

Canada geese 16–17
cape gannets 38, 44–45
caribou 14
cerulean warblers 42
Christmas Island red crabs 11
cottonmouth snakes 8
crustaceans 11, 20–21, 24, 25
curlew sandpipers 43

dangers of migration 12–13, 28,
    38–39, 40, 41, 42–45
diel vertical migration 26–27
dragonflies 14, 16, 32, 33

eels 10
Eleonora's falcons 38
elephants 21, 42
elks 7

emperor penguins 17
emus 35

fish 4, 6, 8, 10–11, 12–13, 14, 18,
    38–39
food, migration for 4, 6–7, 8, 17,
    21, 22, 23, 24, 26, 28, 30, 31,
    32
formations during migration 20–21
frogs 28–29

generational migration 32–33
global warming 44–45

habitat destruction 42, 43
herring 10–11
hibernation 28, 29, 33
hummingbirds 8, 16

insects 9, 14–15, 14–15, 16,
    32–33, 36–37, 44
irruptions 34–35

lobsters 20–21, 24
    spiny lobsters 20–21
locusts 36–37
long-distance migration 30–31
longitudinal migration 22

mammals 4, 5, 6–7, 14, 22–23,
    24–25, 28, 31, 40–41, 42–43,
    44
molt migrations 23
moths 9, 32

navigation 18–19, 28, 30, 32
nomadic birds 34, 35

pelagic red crabs 25
pelicans 20

predators, security from 10, 20, 21,
    23, 24, 25, 26, 29, 38
preparing for migration 14
pronghorns 22

red-breasted nuthatches 34
reptiles 4, 8, 19, 20, 30, 45
routes, migration 16–17

salamanders 28, 29
salmon 12–13, 18, 42, 44
sardines 38
sea lampreys 18
sea turtles 4, 19, 20, 30, 45
    leatherback sea turtles 30
    loggerhead sea turtles 19
seasonal migration 22
sharks 6, 8, 10, 38
    bull sharks 10
    great white sharks 6
    shortfin mako sharks 8
short-distance migration 28–29
snow geese 8–9
snowy owls 34–35
solitary sandpipers 20
songbirds 20, 34, 42, 44
starlings 20, 22
striped bass 10
swans 20, 23

triggers for migration 8, 14, 27

weather, migration for better 4, 7,
    8–9, 16, 22, 32
whales 4, 14, 22–23, 31
white-ruffed manakins 24
wildebeests 5, 40–41, 42, 44
Wilson's phalaropes 23

zooplankton 26–27